Somebody Someday

A Journey of Homelessness, Faith,
& Friendship

Joye Holmes

FIRE MOUNTAIN
PUBLISHING

First Edition, August 2020

Copyright © Joye Holmes and Fire Mountain Publishing (2020)

www.firemountainpublishing.com

ISBN: 978-1-64764-525-0

Library of Congress Control Number: 2020913525

Publisher's Cataloging-in-Publication Data

Name: Holmes, Joye, author.
Title: Somebody , someday : a journey of homelessness , faith , and friendship / Joye Holmes.
Description: First edition | Mansfield, TX: Fire Mountain Publishing, 2020.
Identifiers: LCCN: 2020913525 | ISBN: 978-1-64764-525-0 (pbk.) | 978-1-64764-524-3 (eBook)
Subjects: LCSH Holmes, Joye--Correspondence. | Deaf--United States--Biography. | Homeless men--Correspondence. | Homelessness--United States. | Homeless persons-- United States. | Christian biography. | BISAC BIOGRAPHY & AUTOBIOGRAPHY / People with Disabilities | BIOGRAPHY & AUTOBIOGRAPHY / Personal Memoirs
Classification: LCC HV4505 .H65 2020 | DDC 362.5/20973/092

*To Butch, who taught me much about
compassion and hard work*

Table of Contents

Introduction

AN UNKNOWN HOMELESS MAN ONCE DID ME A FAVOR. Out of that almost-missed moment, a lifetime friendship developed. Before the encounter, I had limited knowledge of the homeless lifestyle and I certainly knew no one who lived it. My days were spent with my suburban family, insulated by space and culture far away from any inner-city struggles. People who lived in those dark, unknown canyons only entered my world through occasional street corner appearances or as stereotypes in some TV police drama.

That naivety changed over the years as I got to know this man better. I saw how he battled daily with problems I rarely even thought about. I learned what saddened him and what brought him joy. I became amazed at his faith, even when he had nothing much more than what he collected that day. I also felt the hurt, when he shrank silently from people by day and when he huddled by himself every night.

Let me share with you through his letters the improbable connection between a middle-class woman in Texas and a homeless man in Georgia. More than that, I want you to see how God worked through this man and how my life was touched by him. He once was merely a label but has since become my friend.

Joye

1 I found your little purse

July 1995

Dear Mrs. Holmes,

Today is Sun. I don't know the date. I collect cans and go from dumpster and just try to survive.

I found your little purse. There was no money in it. I feel bad for you. I am deaf so I don't go thru people. So I am wasting no time sending this to you.

You have a precious family. I have none. But a man does get my mail for me and you be sure to write to me someday. I could use a stamp but thats no big deal.

May God bless you.

Butch

Joye's Notes:

In the summer of 1995, our family was on vacation in Georgia. Arriving in Atlanta on a Saturday night, we checked into a Motel 6 on the Northside. Our itinerary included church and the World of Coca-Cola museum the next day. Because the strap on my purse had broken, I left it in the room while we attended church services that Sunday morning. We only planned to be away for an hour or so. When we returned to our locked room, I was stunned to discover someone had stolen my wallet and sun visor. It was obviously a housekeeper or other staff who was responsible, so we reported the incident to the manager. His only help was advising us to file a police report. That suggestion was impractical since we were leaving early Monday for our home in Arlington, Texas.

I had lost some cash, Six Flags passes, my driver's license, and a credit card. I quickly canceled the card number and planned to take care of the passes at home. Before I was able to finish the process, I received a Comfort Inn envelope from a stranger. In the envelope was a hand-written note on a small yellow piece of paper, along with my credit card, license, and passes. I was surprised anyone would take the time to return my stolen things, much less that the favor originated from a person of the streets. He even politely complimented our family from the photos on the passes, I assumed. I knew he had not taken any money out of the wallet and it did not sound like he wanted anything from me, except perhaps a postage stamp! That seemed like a small request. I sent a little thank-you cash and a few stamps to the return address, never expecting a response. He wrote back.

2 I don't mean to scare you

August 1995

Joye,

Thank you very much for the $10. Nobody has ever done something like that for me before.

I take it from what you said that it seems that your things were stolen out of your room or car or somehow. That is not unusual for that motel. During something called Freaknic, just about all the motels were robbed at gunpoint. I find billfolds and pocketbooks all the time but they are always tore to pieces and nothing in them. I don't mean to scare you. I hope it never happens to you again.

I am fairly intelligent and have had nice relationships with God and some of God's people. On the other hand, a lot of them have hurt me and threw me in reverse. Now in the past year or *so I have really been at peace with myself. I know now that God loves me just the way I am.*

I only had one grandparent and he used to take me to dumps in upstate NY and I learned a lot from him. He lived to 85 yrs old. The other relatives died before my time and my parents died young.

I enjoy doing things at my pace and trying to be happy and working with God. And I'm so glad that you are like that too. In fact, just yesterday at the recycle place a lady who knew I was deaf, told me in writing on paper that her 17 yr. old daughter was real good at sign language. I asked her to bring her daughter next week. She started crying and said her daughter ran away last week and they have not heard from her since. Please tell your children not to do that.

Butch

Joye's Notes:

The second letter from this homeless man, unexpected like the first, was a thoughtful one. Butch thanked me for the $10, somewhat unnecessary since he was the one who had done the favor for me! I have seen plenty of people over the years who could not manage a spoken "Thank You," much less a written one. In fact, I sometimes send gifts for graduation or a wedding without this much acknowledgment in return.

While pleasantly surprised by his expressed gratitude, I was also a bit leery. I did not know what to expect going forward. What kind of person was this? Was he going to ask for more? Maybe those were unfair questions, but I did not know him from Adam, as they say. We have all experienced scams and beggars. One such situation came to my mind. Several years earlier, I had corresponded with some kids under one of those "Adopt a Child" programs. A few years after that ended, a man from Kenya wrote to me, saying he had found a partial envelope with my address on it. He claimed to be a teacher, so I replied. Second and third letters soon arrived with requests for money, so that was that. I did suspect Butch's second letter might be a similar setup. There was no request, but was there going to be a third letter with the real motives?

Why then did I write him back? I do not entirely know. I was raised in a country setting where we always waved at other drivers and acknowledged every person we passed on the street. If someone like Butch takes the time to write, replying seems like the right thing is to do.

I was unacquainted with "Freaknik." I later learned it was an annual spring break gathering in Atlanta, mainly for black college students. It consisted of partying, music, and dancing. Sometimes, rougher stuff went with the fun.

3 Even the bees like me

September 1995

Joye and Jenna,

What a life I have now. Its starting to get dark but that has lifted my spirits too.

How is Jennas rabbits. I think you said something one time about some pets. I just love animals. A lot more than people. There is a Mexican heap yard on my turf, it's a spooky place, a bunch of garages, all kinds of junks and so forth that are hot, and anyways, they pretend that they are mechanics and so forth, I go there every day and they enjoy seeing me and giving me cans, ect. and they have a little Banty rooster all the way from Mexico. I cuddle up to him.

I would like to be more free around them but I have always hated booze with a passion. Thats all I've seen all my life and it sends chills up my back. So I don't hang around nobody. But Atlanta is one big joke and so its hard for Jesus to get a word in edgewise. I'm just glad He reached out to me thru you.

I couldn't see any reason to try real hard to live. I've been trapped in a dumpster more than once and lifted up by the truck because I didn't hear it coming. Once, I remember reading the driver's lips when he discovered I was in the dumpster. He said, "Your lucky." If he had used the "scoop," I would have been thrown into the belly of the truck and would have been squashed. He had squashed people before! I didn't know why God spared my life. Now I do and I try harder now. I even appreciate the rain because I never wear a shirt and the rain gets me pretty clean. I've never had a bath or shower in many years.

A Chinese dentist is going to work on my teeth free. I go in a Chinese complex too every day. They are real weird.

Well, I guess the moon is beckoning me. I can drop off in a minute. I've had a good day and this letter and thinking of you all makes me feel good. Even the bee's like me. I did have a near death experience with a full hive of bees but since then anything that stings me doesn't bother me. I get *in with 100's of them every day. God bless them. And God bless you. With all my love.*

Butchy

Also Miss Joye the ring is for Jenna. I just found it hot diggity dog.

Joye's Notes:

A third letter did come, followed by hundreds more over the next twenty-five years. Each letter I received from Butch seemed to unfold another detail about him or a long-hidden secret from his world. I have included a small selection of his letters in this book, because I want to share his story with you. The letters will give you, in his own words, a picture of Butch and a unique life that is on-the-other-side-of-the-moon different from mine.

Butch normally mailed letters to me, but he would also send cards or clippings he had uncovered in the garbage. I was a little afraid to hang onto some of the correspondence because it arrived at times with garbage smells and stains. Occasionally, I would receive some added treasure he had collected. On this occasion, he enclosed a ring to my daughter Jenna. It was one he had found, probably in a recent birthday goody bag. He shared the repurposed gift with a child-like exuberance that I have come to expect from him.

4 What good is soap on an empty stomach?

September 1995

Hi Joye Precious and all the beautiful faces in the pictures,

Right off I can't help but tell you what a fondness I have for the name Vern. I grew up in the most poor rural area that I have yet to see. I have known this one and that one to live in trees, in cardboard boxes, barn lofts, but the closest thing I ever met to living in my imagination of what it was like many many years ago for poor people, was a very old man named Vern Frink. And he lived to be in the late 80's and he was never sick. He always lived in a junk car way out in a field.

I will tell you Joye that this very morning when I went to the Reynolds Recycle Trailer and I am always there way before it opens, and there was Mexicans sleeping everywhere right on parking lot *pavements. Many sleep all around a church next to the supermarket. They just lay newspapers or cardboard down and make a bed. I just live similarly only I usually sleep in a vehicle. But 2 or 3 hrs sleep is fine with me. Then I sweep, mop, do this and that at the QT where you probably stopped. I get free gas, I could eat if I wanted to. I drink a lot of Cappacuni coffee and put popcorn in every cup. I love popcorn. But I never ate a square meal in years. An besides, I'm always alone and I guess I am a dissident because I don't know what it is to have a close family or sit down at a table with other people.*

I am glad you talk to me about God and His love and word. I found a cap that said Church of Christ on it. I have heard of your church. As for me, I have been very hurt time and time again. People in GA churches make me sick. I would go and try to make friends and they would bring the next week bags of soap and health supplies. I can't stand high and mighty people and I am not filthy. I know you are not like that. What good is soap on a hungry stomach and not one church member has ever gave me a bite to eat. Unfortunately, I guess my only grandfather probably went to hell because he went to church one time and they made fun of him and he never went again.

The only thing I miss a family attachment or any kind of attachment. But I am starting to come out of the cave because of you. I hope Vern is teaching your children martial arts. You can never be too sure today. Please pray for my arm, my teeth, and for my strength. Bye Joye, Vern and children.

Butch

Joye's Notes:

What good is soap on an empty stomach? Indeed! I have, on more than one occasion, been on the giving end of the "church-to-poor" handout. With good, though sometimes misguided, intentions we rally at Christmas or Thanksgiving to gather and distribute baskets. When we help the poor or homeless, the occasional handouts are often comprised of trinkets or items we assume they need. Since Butch was on the receiving end of similar endeavors, his perspective was enlightening to me. Passing out gift packages is fine, but it is a different story for benefactors to become more involved with another person from that world. There are people, God bless them, who do make such sacrifices, but the numbers must be relatively small. As the saying goes, is it better to give someone a fish or teach them how to fish? Giving fish or soap, while admirable, has its limitations.

It is a very sad commentary on churches when we treat any visitor with such simple neglect or even meanness. The damage is compounded if he or she never again attempts to connect with God. That one-time encounter may affect not only them and their spiritual relationship but also possibly that of their children or grandchildren. I do not know the circumstances of what happened with Butch's grandfather nor do I know his actions at the time. The one group you would expect to be accepting and forgiving had scorned him. The church should be the most welcoming place in the world and yet many surveys show that one of the most common reasons for avoiding or leaving the church is that people do not feel accepted there! Tragedy.

My husband's name is Gary. I can only surmise Butch got confused because I had earlier mentioned my sister, Verna. Regardless, Gary was Vern for a while.

5 I have never felt worthy

October 1995

Hi Momma Joye and Vern and family,

I thank my God upon every remembrance of you.
God has been so good to me. I dont want to ever
lose your friendship. I hope to evolve into a better
person and be at peace with the deepest part of
my soul within a year. That is my goal.

I have always lived in turmoil and betrayal, abuse,
and unloved but I have begun to open up to
butterflys, cats, dogs, and a big rat. I see him now
and then and he's a pretty good guy. If I was to
ever go to a church I think it would have to be one
that I could worship God in a very deep way and
talk to Him. I have never felt worthy.

I'm really excited about what I'm going to eat for
my supper tonite. I found it in a dumpster and it
was a carryout not even touched, a Mexican chili

with cheese, tortilla chips, it must be 5 dollars. I really have warm feelings for Mexican people, native Indians and Latin Americans if I know what they are. I'm not sure. I never go into a store or home so I find all my food and I think the Mexicans leave some food out for me. And I believe God specially loves those people and the state of Texas.

Be careful this Holloween.

Love,

Butch

Joye's Notes:

They say life has its simple pleasures. Honestly, though, it is hard to comprehend how a discarded takeout meal pulled from a dumpster can be one of them. Even if it is Mexican food! Note that this take-out from the trash was not warmed in a microwave either. There are always reminders of how big the gulf is between our lives. A warm meal served on a plate takes on a new meaning for me.

Butch has his prejudices and opinions on a variety of subjects, including views on other groups of people. Those opinions seemed to vary and change over time, just as ours sometimes do. For the most part, he generally expressed a favorable view of "Mexicans." On several occasions, he has mentioned good treatment he had received from them. There was one unnamed couple from Mexico he knew for a few years, ever since they had first arrived. Butch enjoyed watching their family grow, until one day they were gone. He appreciated their hard work and I think he related to their struggle to make it in life.

6 Kids throw rocks at me

July 1996

Dear Joye and family,

I am sitting in my truck, raining very hard and been thinking about you all. I am OK. I did break some stuff inside my left foot about a month ago. It is not now killing me like it was. I hope in another month it will be over. I didn't go to no Doctor. Never do. My body isn't a beauty spectacle. I've got lots of cuts and a big gash where kids throw rocks at me.

I like to scan over health magazines or Good Housekeeping, stuff like that to see the food sections. I never knew corn was good for your heart so lately I been eating some corn on the cob. I see them in dumpsters all the time. I never use to eat corn. I go for things that don't make me full or gain weight.

I am still doing a lot of thinking about how to make the can collecting easier for me and also how to guarantee that no bags go flying off my truck in strong winds and stuff. You just don't know the feeling when people on 285 smash into a big bag of cans and they scatter everywhere and all that work down the drain. I have a tendency to really get down on myself when life throws me a curve. But the little things I worry about don't compare to the story I read last nite about Annette Funicello the Mouseketeer who has M..S. and I doubt is going to live much longer. You pray for her but don't forget my foot if you can.

I hope your family is fine and your mother.

Love,

Butch

Joye's Notes:

Butch loved to read. Granted, it was usually magazines and newspapers found among the garbage. He also read discarded books. Once, he was thrilled to find a tossed Christian book that had been signed by the author. He could not understand, though, how someone would let a treasure like that go.

At first, I was surprised to see a homeless person so concerned with health. I should not have been since we universally prefer to keep living well. Some of us are better at maintaining health than others. For the homeless, there is so little real access to health care. Sure, there are emergency rooms, but how do they obtain the education and tools to remain healthy? Many do not even have transportation. Butch's health plan came almost entirely from magazine articles. Corn is good for you? Then eat more corn on the cob. There is plenty around if you know where to look. I am not sure why he worried about gaining weight. He must have weighed less than 125 pounds, soaking wet.

His story about Annette Funicello is moving. He daily struggles to survive and yet he has such a tender heart for the pain and suffering of others, even for strangers. Some people might think the idea of a homeless person showing such thoughtful compassion for a Mouseketeer is strange. I found it compelling. Of course, even as he asked for prayers for her, he added that I must not forget his feet. Remember, even Jesus was reminded to throw the dogs a bone! (Funicello announced in 1992 she had been diagnosed with multiple sclerosis years earlier. She died of complications from the disease in 2013.)

It breaks my heart when Butch loses a day's labor because cans are blown off the truck. He is a hard worker who starts his job long before daylight. Besides, he got paid so little for collecting trash tossed by others. To have a day's work disappear must have been devastating.

7 I didn't commit suicide

August 1996

Dearest Joye and Jenna,

Just read your warmly letter. I now have a sense of belonging to somebody. You all are my kind of people. I don't relate or open up to anybody. I have always coped with depression. But I'm more positive now than ever before. Each day I see things that make me more thankful.

There is so much that is hard for me to accept. The food waste of the Olympic personnel is beyond your imagination. They get tons of carryout's free and throw it away. I have no sympathy for the homeless either because it is so easy to survive here that its uncomparable but they would rather be a scourge and it is out of control. It is sad that people everywhere around here don't absorb the fact that God loves them and He is worthy to be praised.

I read about a month ago about the hot dry weather where you are. I always kept that on my mind. Weather doesn't get me all bent out of shape like when I was growing up in central NY. I dreaded every day. I am so glad I didn't commit suicide. It was always on my mind.

I'm even going to be wearing some police clothes soon. Ha ha. The cops here staying at the Ramada threw some out but they took the patches off which I'm glad for. I am not good with sizzors. I also think I'm finally satisfied with sunglasses. I have found a zillion this year but I am very fussy about wearing the very best for my particular eyes and all I ever find is worthless to me but I have found 2 good pair this week. Wow! I bet they are from out of state. Bye Bye

Butchy

Joye's Notes:

Envelopes came addressed to "Yellow Rose of Texas," "A Joye to Know Holmes," "I'm Jumpin' for Joye Holmes," or whatever was on Butch's mind. Pen colors changed constantly. Discarded stationary of every description was abundant for Butch, of course. Here is an actual sample of one of his letters. This one was written upside-down on a repurposed calendar page.

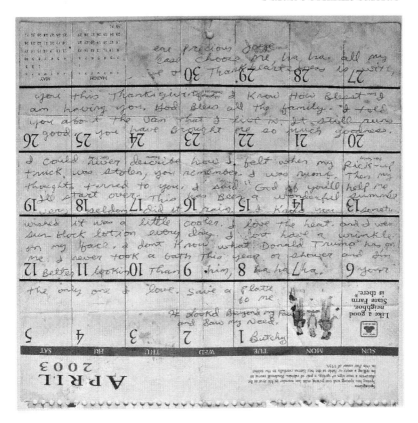

Figure 1 Letter from Butch

Writing to Butch or anyone, especially over an extended time, is difficult for me. Like many people, I do not feel like I have much to write home about. One can only say so much concerning family, the weather, and vacation plans. My job as an accountant did not supply much fodder for sharing, as you might imagine. Butch seemed to enjoy very much hearing about my family. Gary and I have two children who grew up, as it were, before his eyes. Wade was involved in baseball and other sports while Jenna was interested in various activities, especially anything that involved people. I always thought Butch seemed most concerned about Jenna and her safety. Twenty years after we started writing, when he was asking about the kid's post-high school life, he confessed that Jenna was, indeed, his favorite.

8 If I could cry for you I would

September 1996

Beloved,

I also grew up doing farm work. I worked my tail off on a bunch of farms in upstate N.Y. and was lucky if I got paid. Usually around 5 dollars a day. I have always been frugal, and grateful. If I see a penny, I'll take my gloves off and pick it up. I get a thrill out of finding a quarter in a payphone. I check all of them every day and I collect change from car wash vacuums cause they like me to clear out the dirt. I might find 25 or 30 cents. Any money is money to me. Nobody ever took care of me all my life. I am very honest about that.

My elders were all hunters, fishers and outlaws and they made me go coon hunting almost every nite. Theres nothing like digging thru bushes, prickers, you name it. I've known a lot of suffering. And I hated going into beer joints and waiting on them. I was always shy and unhappy. All my relatives were hell raisers and hit all the salloons all the time. So I have never drank or smoked. I am still trying to analyze who I am and where I fit in with this world. Nobody claims me, and lots of times I felt God let me down but He has ways of evening the score.

I'm sorry Joye. I can't tell you how much your last letter meant to me. You and your mother. I am a little puzzled how your mother can be 89 yrs old. I'm not exactly sure what she's got but its been so long since I've been around somebody old or sick that I don't cry or equate with somebodys ordeals. But if I could cry for you I would.

Hey, maybe this is the year for the Rangers. I hope so. And I hope Wade becomes a pro. player. They can ship all those sorry Latins back and make baseball fun again. Anybody ever spit in my face today would meet his maker.

Butchy

Joye's Notes:

In many ways, Butch and I are very different. My life in suburbia as a wife, mother, church member, and accountant contrasted sharply with Butch's solitary life of dumpster-diving at the fringe of the city. Yet, we are all children of God and we can probably find something we have in common with most folks. That can be small at first and may be difficult to discover. In time, as we get to know someone and enjoy some sort of relationship, then the common elements may grow as one or both sides pick up interests of the other.

Butch and I both grew up with very little, although he was much worse off than I was. My childhood included water wells, outhouses, and saving scraps for the chickens. I pulled cotton every year from the time I was eight through high school graduation. School closed just for that purpose in late summer and early fall. The meager earnings went for school clothes, so I was glad about that. However, I vowed two things during those days: I would never marry a farmer and I would never pass up a glass of water.

The times were hard for me, but I had a family that loved me and cared for me. I enjoyed good health and friends in my small school and the equally small church. But still, we were quite poor, and that experience created a thread between Butch and me that others might not share. Sure, my life of poverty was long-gone, but the experiences and memories linger on and likely gave Butch and me some sort of commonality. I do not search payphones for change, but I still pick up every penny or quarter I find. Maybe frugality grew out of my childhood experience. It is always nice to find something in common with another soul. If nothing more, it helped me to have something to write.

I was not sure I could trust Butch on everything he wrote at first, but I quickly sensed sincerity. I was relieved early on to hear he did not drink the original $10 away. It was his to do as he pleased, but we always like to envision any gift to a "poor" person as destined for milk and bread rather than Smirnoff's. I know all homeless are not alcoholics and drug addicts, but apparently, there are enough people in those situations to keep fueling broad bias.

Butch always was interested in my friends and extended family. He would ask about my mother and her years of dealing with Alzheimer's. In contrast, it is somewhat sad that I have face-to-face friends who cannot even name my two children, much less my mom or siblings.

Over time, Butch adopted the Texas Rangers as his team. As for me, I would not send all foreign-born baseball players back to their home countries, of course. Roberto Alomar might be the lone exception. I was not a fan of that umpire-spitting stunt he pulled.

9 I just feel good all over

January 1997

Joye, Gary, Wade, Jenna,

Happy N.Y. to a truly cheezy family. I'm alive and gonna be whole hog for 97. I just feel good all over. Well, I do think my home sweet home truck needs alignment but that Mexican garage will do it for me free. I don't see them every day but they save cans for me and every time I stop it's a sweet reunion. They have a place in their heart for me. Most Americans give me ulcers.

My viewmaster collection is now picking up. I found The Batman, Cinderella, Hunchback, and The Lion King. I'm just tickled pink. I also found a beautiful rose in a plastic wrap like they sell in stores but I keep it in the truck. And for Christmas I found a big apple coated with chocolate and nuts real thick. And also some kind of big kidney beans cooked sweet and sour I believe.

As for the big Thitey, it is same ole stuff—five murders Christmas Day. And the T.V. is trying to teach people how to use 911. People will call to see if a turkey is done. Do you ever get audited. I have never filed taxes.

Write again when you can.

Butch

Joye's Notes:

"NY" is for New Year's Day. "Thitey" is his joke for the city. Butch likes to play with words. It also becomes quickly evident he employees a rather random style of writing, skipping from thought to thought with abandonment.

He had found a kid's View-Master earlier and was thrilled. He said he was giving himself a Christmas present. It is heartbreaking that his few possessions and treasures were periodically stolen. Who steals from a homeless person? Who understands thieves anyway? Someone else has something they want, so they decide I will just take it because I can.

I had explained that Gary was a CPA who prepared taxes, but I think Butch has never quite grasped the concept of what Gary did. There were so many things in my life that were never a part of Butch's sphere. That made relating to him difficult at times, so I limited my time writing about those things that might seem too unfamiliar.

10 Bone cold

February 1997

Miss Joye,

The weather has been unreal. So I duck into car washes and they are a good place to sleep. I'm doin my best to ride the freeze out. Mostly my hands freeze no matter what I put on. But I use the blowers in restrooms and just hang tough.

I do have a problem at a complex I go in to get cans. A man has a Rottewiller and he likes to come up on me with the dog and laughs saying sickem. He holds it on a leash but I'm afraid of dogs and I can't talk so he must think it's a joke. I might just feed the dog a nice steak with some "special seasonin."

I went to sleep last Thanksgiving nite and woke up a few hours later and on my hood was a bag with 3 plates of food. I thot maybe the angel got the wrong address. As for the chocolate cookies, only

God knows how much I love chocolate. When I was a little boy I had to really grin & bare it cause the cupboards were usually empty. One morning just before the bus, I saw what I thot was a candy bar. Of course it was Ex Lax and I ate all of them, and I will never forget that day. I missed the bus that afternoon & had to walk all the way home. ½ dead.

Give everyone a hug for me, the dog, cat, Wade, Jenna, the Avon lady, on and on. That was my 1st job when I was a little boy, selling Stanley Home stuff. I rode my bike to Tim Buk Too.

Bone cold. I thank God for the sleeping bag you sent me.

Breaker 1-9,

Butch

Joye's Notes:

Think about how cold it gets sitting in an unheated vehicle for an hour. I can only imagine what it is like trying to spend all night in a truck or automobile during the winter months. They are notoriously poorly insulated. I am sure hand dryers were not placed in gas station restrooms to serve as heaters for those without, but I guess it works to some extent.

Occasionally, I would send Butch something that might help him with the elements, such as socks or gloves. For this Christmas, I had mailed him a sleeping bag. It must have helped him, since he later remarked it was the first time he had slept for 14 hours.

I am thankful never to have experienced what Butch did, but love of chocolate is something he and I have in common. I still long for one of my mother's chocolate pies, the very best there ever were. I have not been able to duplicate her pies. She always explained the recipe by saying, "a handful of this and a bit of that."

I cannot grasp why anyone, especially an adult, would think scaring another person with a vicious dog constitutes fun. I can never get my head around the meanness and brutality we humans are capable of inflicting on other people. It is likely cruel to feed the Rottweiler a steak with "special seasoning," but there is a macabre sort of humor to the idea.

11 I hope I'm a somebody someday

November 1998

Mom, folks,

There is a restaurant just up the road from where I sleep every nite. Its called "Folks." I just love its dumpster. I'll go up there 3 or 4 in the morning before the truck comes. No place is better than that place. I sleep out back behind the Chevron on Windy Hill Rd.

Nobody has ever read a story to me in my entire life, And I was born April 4, 1957 so I don't know how many years that is but a long time. But I do remember many years ago there was a Gospel song "Somebodys out there." I hope I'm a somebody someday.

I'm getting in the fishin mood. The last time I went, I fell in the water 3 times. No, I wasn't drunk. But I found this herb medicine in a *dumpster called Molotonin and I thought it was a vitamin. Wow. I've done so many stupid things I ought to write a book. Probably nobody has ever zipped their fly up and caught it in the zipper. Somebody had to help me.*

Have yourself a big chocklate smoothie and smiles for me.

Butch

Joye's Notes:

Butch is always busting common stereotypes. It is easy to depict all homeless people as lazy panhandlers. However, Butch was an extremely hard worker. Even though living about as simple of a life as one can, he was an entrepreneur. He conducted a business that helped him and benefitted society. At times, he would think and plan how he could improve his production. He had to discover outlets for his product. He got excited when the price of recycled aluminum rose and dejected when the price fell. He had to adjust when market outlets closed. In those respects, he is no different than the rest of us, trying to support ourselves.

Sometimes Butch's letters seemed more random than usual and he seemed peppier. He always denied the use of alcohol and drugs and I had no reason to doubt him. However, I think he would self-medicate to treat many of his aches and pains. Like finding his food in dumpsters, he also found all kinds of medicine. It is a miracle he did not kill himself. Melatonin is a hormone that is used to treat sleep disorders. One main side effect is dizziness, which Butch experienced in the fishing episode.

What does it mean to be a somebody? We usually think it involves being important. In simplest terms, being somebody means we are important to at least one other person. We want to be known by them and important in their eyes. Unfortunately, people exist who we might say are nobodies, unknown really by another soul. They live and die in obscurity, alone and unmissed. I do hope Butch can feel someone else does care for him and he is truly a somebody.

12 Wonderful experience and that was in a dumpster

May 1999

Precious Joye,

Since your last letter I've had boo boos, one real bad slash. I just don't want to go into it, you couldn't handle it. It completely cut my achilles tendon. But I'm too small for crutches and after a week, I was hobbilling pretty good, 3 weeks, I was myself again. God is so good.

I only had one sister that lived. The other one died in her sleep. Anyways, Norma Jean was raped when she was 11 and had the baby, Jay. Jay has been in a institution all his life, I haven't seen no relatives in maybe 30 years. I may be the only one out of maybe 400 relatives that got down on my knees and had a wonderful experience, and that was in a dumpster.

So I see all kinds of people every day and then I never see them again. But I see my cats every nite. Theres 3 of em. They are stray, they never get close to me, but I put a dish for food and a dish for water a little ways from my truck.

This motorcycle couple pass thru this way on holidays I can't believe they like me but they stop every time to see me. Her name is Alpha. Her twin is Omega. Don't worry, I'm confused too. So that's me in the picture with her. But I's glad they talk to me. They even hug me and kiss me on the cheek. I's not used to that.

Butch

Joye's Notes:

I can relate to the "too small for crutches" statement. I am short too at 5 feet and have had to use crutches. Doctors need to realize some adults need kid-sized crutches!

Butch always seemed to like animals and pets. Perhaps it is that quality that shone through early and made him seem less suspicious or threatening. Can a person who loves animals be mean?

It was four years of writing before I saw a photograph of Butch. Since he has no camera, I only have a few photos from him. Of course, my mind had already created an image of him. Therefore, I was surprised that he was white. It probably says something about my own bias that I assumed he was African American, I guess because he was living in Atlanta. I know, that is not fair, but we do stereotype. In my defense, it made no difference whether he was black or white.

Figure 2 Butch and Alpha with Truck

There are so many things I have learned from Butch about the life of a homeless person. In this letter, he talked about seeing many people, but most of them he never sees again. Think about a life where all relationships are only temporary. Without family, without neighbors, without workplace associates, without churches or associations, there can hardly be anything that we would consider long-term. How hard it must be to make friends when you have no home and live in a world of silence. Yes, I cried when this motorcycle friend kissed him on the cheek. So fleeting. So random. Yet that is about all he has known. I am so happy to be able to share his friendship for these many years. I hope it gives him some great comfort too.

13 Not a popular name in Georgia

June 1999

Well, How Bout Them Holmes!

I have to keep my name a secret, ha ha, "Sherman" That's not a popular name in Georgia. My middle name is Wayne. I think my parents were drunk when they named me but all my relatives` had a nickname and I didn't know my real name for many years. Everybody called me Butch. You have a beautiful name.

As for my writing ability, ha ha. I, as you know, was not born in a religious environment. I can write well and convey thoughts simply because I didn't go deaf until 10 or 11. I was abused and my head took a lot of fists. If you came up behind me, I might jump 10 feet.

I ride down this one rural lane every now and then. There is one house where an old man lives with his 35 or so yr. old daughter. She is feeble minded but a wonderful person. The other day I cleaned their gutters. Then, a school bus came round the bend and stopped to let the neighborhood kids off. She stood there and watched. Every day she stands out there and watches for the bus. She had never went to school. Tears rolled down my face. I've always loved deaf people and those who could use a miracle.

Well, I use to and still do see lots of vitamins, pills, all kinds of junk I found but very few are worth a flip. If I see any fruit, I'll suck the juice. I like to chew on bagels and after a while spit it out. Can you imagine in all my 41 yrs I never knew what a bagel was. And when I did start seeing them advertised, I thot they were for Jews. So I guess I'm a little bit Jewish now. But I do like oatmeals if I ever find any. If you feel like sending me a couple oatmeal packages if they will fit in a envelope, that would be nice but I can get by.

Butch

Joye's Notes:

I am surprised at how articulate Butch can be at times. Sure, the spelling and grammar were not always there, but you can tell he does read. His vocabulary often is broader than mine. It is easy to view people with limited formal education as less smart, which is not true. I know that from my own parents who only went through 8th and 10th grades

I did send Butch some packages of oatmeal at this point and later as well. He seemed to get a real kick out of those tidbits. He never asked for much and, over the years, I sent him very little really. Besides small things like stamps or oatmeal, I only remember him once requesting unprompted for anything specific. He wanted a shirt. He sent me a swatch of cloth, saying he liked that particular type of material. I did my best to find a similar fabric and mailed him two shirts for Christmas. The gifts I sent were nearly always for either Christmas or his birthday, just as I do for my family. I did not want to view our relationship as a charity project. Sometimes there would be a bit of money, but I never thought he would use it unwisely. For example, I remember once he took some of the money to open a post office box for a while.

After five years of knowing Butch, I discovered his real name. However, he seems like a Butch to me. I am sure Atlanta has not forgotten Sherman's March to the Sea and its destruction of the city and homes at the end of the Civil War. In Ken Burns Civil War documentary an older lady from Mississippi said, "Our family never cared for Mr. Lincoln." I bet some of the citizens of Atlanta never cared for Mr. Sherman.

For me, this scene of the 35-year-old woman standing outside each day waiting to wave at the bus is so haunting and sad. The emotion intensifies when you add in the lonely observer to the mix. Truly, we need to love all those that could use a miracle.

14 Oh sweet Suzie

July 2000

God bless you Momma Joye,

It didn't take me long to get your "hip" celebration letter. I have never in my life had a person "want" to love me, just really think I'm special and make it a point to always be there for me. Not one. No one has ever sent. me a celebration letter, you can take that to the bank.

A funny thing happened yesterday. I was in a dumpster in a alley by that river on Franklin Rd. All of a sudden a hot lookin car pulls up, the dude jumps out and runs. 2 motorcycle cops pull up, jump off and try to run, but they both were over 200 lbs. I jump outta da dumpster and take off after the dude. He tries to get cross the river and sees me comin, runs back up the hill and the cops nail him,. Ha ha. Oh sweet Suzie.

Right now I am winning the battle against a straff infection in both legs. I was mowing a lawn and got poison ivy bad. Of course I couldn't go to a doctor. But I always save all the herbs I find. People move, throw everything away. I took several things. I had teeth problems that hurts too. I never saw the "Survivors"? on TV of course. But they are all sissys. I would like to see them jump in a dumpster and stare face to face with 2 hugh raccoons on their back legs fixin to attack. They missed me by a hair.

Butch

Joye's Notes:

I do not know what had possessed Butch to go chasing a suspect for the police. Such is a day in the life of a homeless person!

Several books have been written by or about people who were homeless temporarily, maybe for a couple of years or a few months. In fact, some authors only went through the experience for a few weeks. I will not minimize those experiences, because even one night on the streets is not something I desire. However, Butch's homelessness stretched over thirty years, a huge chunk of his adult life. He had to know how to survive for decades and that is something I respect about him.

When I think about jumping into a dumpster, which I never do, I think about the yucky food and goo. I forget about the ants, bees, roaches, rats, and mice that might be met. I can see how it would be scary to stare down a pair of angry raccoons in a tight box. I suppose the three of them were fighting over the good stuff.

15 No cover, no truck, what a life

May 2001

Dearest Lover of Jesus,

The skys are pitch black-mid-day, pouring down. No cover, no truck, what a life. I've had 3 vehicles stolen in this crazy town. There is no fear of God here. I'm just now starting to have visions of someday having a job, having wheels again, and maybe goin to church again, maybe eatin right, maybe getting a haircut, just a few off the wall thoughts. But I'll never live "inside." You remember when I used to get bad cuts and gashes, the homeless clinics would zip me to Grady Hosp where they use homeless people for experiments, ha ha. I'd stay just long enough to get ½ way fixed and sneak out.

I don't know much of whats goin on in the world. I know the ghetto news. But everybody stays in *the woods when its hot. Even naked I'm sorry to say. But I circulate so much, from 4 in the morn to midnite sometimes, that I keep tabs on the gang and a lot of people know "Butch.' I even saw a new "girl," female if you please, on the street the other day. Never saw her before. She was sramblin for cig. butts fat cats dropped. Maybe get 3 or 4 more drags. God bless her.*

Mary, the old lady who pulls a wagon, her dog pulls her, runs up to me now and then to shoot some bull. I put my hand on her shoulder, she crys I gonna be OK Butch, OK. Sure Mary. On behalf of Mary, Pee Wee, Toby, Karla, Jo Jo, Skeeter, least of all me, may the Good Lawd bless.

Butch

Joye's Notes:

Three stolen vehicles. Do we know what it is like to have our entire home and all our possessions periodically burned to the ground?

From what I understand, Atlanta had about 3,500-4,000 shelterless people at that time. Although there are always new theories offering solutions, the real goal in most cities seems to be control and containment, rather than elimination, of the problem. When we think of the homeless, we often wrestle with motivations. Are people there out of choice or because they have no other options? The answers must be complex because each case is different. Certainly, with Butch, there was a choice to some degree. He had stated he did not want to be in a house, and he did tend to shy away from people. On the other hand, considering the abuse that has been afflicted on him, his early life with a dysfunctional family, his lack of family ties, his limited formal education, and his deafness, there can be a strong argument that he has few options. Yes, he faced deep despair and desperation, but there was also hope. Where there is a possibility for betterment, including a real job, a church community, and a haircut, there is a spark of hope. It is too easy for us to say all homeless are there by choice and could get out if they want. On the flip side, those things do apply to some people. Help from the outside is complicated and hard, or else there would not be so much homelessness.

It was good to see Butch did have some connections with people in the homeless community. Deep and permanent friendships eluded him, but it is nice for him to relate with people in the same boat.

16 Talk about winning the lottery

December 2001

My Joye,

I am sittin here in a Waffle House so I can see better to write. For some reason, I think better at night. And then I will walk back to my "house," ha ha... the old junk I sleep in, cuddle up in my new sleeping bag, shed a few tears, and fall asleep thinking about what a angel you are.

I never went to school long. But I never had a friend because I was so poor and skinny and kept to myself. I never dreamed that using a stamp that I found in a dumpster, sending somebody stuff I found in a pocketbook, would turn my life completely around. Talk about winning the lottery.

I came from a area in upstate NY, everybody was wild, alcoholic, and life was just day to day survival. I was born out of wedlock and was never wanted. So, from abuse and bad nerves and fear, I went nerve deaf very early. I went to school for 2 yrs to learn to lip read and sign. When I found your pocketbook I was at one of the lowest depressions of my life and suicide was not far away. All I want to do now is live for you, and God.

Did I tell you I have this muffler shop that let's me keep my cans there so nobody steals them. An I have finally made friends with a beautiful black cat that I pet, hold, and may keep if it doesn't belong to anybody. This is the 1st one. I would love to keep him in my sleeping bag with me. I never wanted to tell you, I've froze many times.

Love,

Butch

Joye's Notes:

Remember, Butch lived without electricity or lights and got up for work long before daybreak. Therefore, he usually went to sleep when it grew dark. Sometimes, though, Butch parked under a streetlight, to write a letter or read.

I had sent another sleeping bag because the first one had been stolen from him. Butch was always so expressive with gratitude. I did so little for him, yet he could make me feel important. What greater honor can be received than to have someone say you are their angel? Who knows what a little kindness may do for another person?

I did not realize Butch had found the postage stamp when he sent that first letter to me, but it makes sense. Other people's discards supplied many of his needs. One man's trash is indeed another man's treasure. I suppose he could have been pen pals with other people during these years, but I had no sign of that. More than once, Butch mentioned he never returned anybody else's stolen things to them. I believed that God intervened at that moment years earlier when Butch took the effort of first writing to me and returning my credit card and other stolen items.

Even though we may not be around the homeless too much, we can at least grasp some of the difficulties they face. Likewise, we are aware of the struggles that the disabled encounter. We may not realize how many people must climb both mountains. It is about four times more likely for a disabled person to be homeless than it is for an able-bodied person. Contributing to the battle is the lack of help and facilities. For example, while there are thousands of homeless shelters and community housing projects across the United States, less than a hand full cater to the deaf.

17 God and a Coke delivery man helped me

July 2002

Hi Everyone,

How is things in Texas. Whew is it hot & dry.
Maybe tomorrow or any day before you get this
Lord willing, just maybe it may change. It may get
115 this summer. I'm not upset when it gets real
hot.

Thank you so much for the lovely card. I don't go
to church. But I'll keep my eyes open for a church
like yours. But I know this state in and out. If
somebody started a church with the name
Hypocrite on it, it would be full in no time.

I got a hold of some poison ivy but God and a Coke
delivery man helped me get better. He comes
over to my car sometimes to check on me. It was
all over my face and my eyes were almost shut.
His wife is a nurse and he called her and she got

me a very good medicine and it immediately started clearing up.

I just found a 1995 yearbook from Pebblebrook H.S. Not 1 girl in that whole senior class was as pretty as Jenna. Some of em scared me, ha ha.

Love,

Butchy

Joye's Notes:

A few months earlier someone had given Butch a station wagon. That kindness, as well as the help from the Coke delivery man and his wife, illustrate Butch did meet many people who had aided him over the years. Sometimes that came from churches, clinics, or food banks, but many times individuals have extended helping hands. That could be giving him a vehicle, repairing a truck, leaving out food, offering him a little job, stopping to say hi and take his picture, letting him get mail at the house, giving him a little extra for his cans, letting him use the restroom facilities or warm himself a bit, letting him park his truck at night, or allowing him to refill his cup. Some people treated him badly, but there were many more who showed random acts of kindness. Jesus talked of the blessing of giving a cup of cold water in his name. People indeed offered that very blessing to Butch, and I am so thankful.

18 I didn't know if it was water or my tears

October 2002

Precious Joye, Jenna, Gary and Wade,

I can just imagine how busy your home is. Just don't tell anybody about me. They'll think your loco or somethin.

The weathers holdin up pretty good. I don't feel the cold till I'm numb, ha ha. But being inside a car sure is a blessing. I've slept on the ground in winters with freezing water drownin me. I didn't know if it was water or my tears.

I've been so happy this year with all the news from you. You won't find too many Christians like Jenna and Wade up here. I stare at their pictures all the time. I have no idea what happened to those motorcycle people who took pictures of me. Very strange. I would guess he was well over 400 lbs. Biggest man I ever saw. He may have died.

I sure hope Jenna's foot is gettin better. I just know how painful that is. Over the years, dropping something heavy, or jumping out of a dumpster way too high off the ground, I've broke toes in both feet. I understand broken toes never heal. So I wear 3 or 4 pair of socks. Believe it or not, I come across many thrown away pairs of shoes every day and week. It might take 100 pair before I find ones that my feet like.

Let me know if theres anything I can do for you and Gary and all. I can easily collect coupons and other stuff out of dumpsters.

Butchy

Joye's Notes:

I cannot fathom trying to live in a car or truck as my house, but that must be better than nothing. Butch did have his share of sleeping in the open.

When Jenna was in high school, she had surgery on both feet. That is what he is referring to. Butch's constant struggle with aches and pains is a reminder of the blessing we have with good available health care.

I was disheartened to hear of the motorcycle couple who were no longer coming around. As Butch related earlier, he gets to know people for brief periods and then never sees them again. A homeless person could just vanish as if they never existed. My only contact information for Butch was an ever-changing address of an unknown person. If anything happened to him, there might not be any trace of him and probably no notification to me. It makes me think of when Jenna had a pet cat for over seven years. I never considered myself a pet person, but relationships with pets do develop. One day, the cat disappeared forever and now that simple relationship seems a bit unfinished. I still find myself looking twice when I see another grey tabby cat, wondering if it might be Buttons. The thought that people we are close to could just end like that was troublesome.

19 *I did it for the baby*

May 2003

Miss Joye,

*Your one prayer did come true. Just after I got
your letter, the next day and I was feeling sad, I
get that way sometimes. I guess the word is
insignificant and I was sort of swamped by all
kinds of people wantin me to do stuff for them for
nothin. I sat down under a tree by myself away
from the world, my head hangin down, and then I
saw somethin out of the corner of my eye. There
was the most beautiful red Cardinal bird I ever
saw. They don't get real pretty here in GA. But
this one came right out of a magazine. I almost
cryed thinkin of you and your letter. I got up a
better man and kissed my insignificance goodbye.*

*It seems like someone in your family has a
birthday or something. I am sorry if I forgot. My
mind has been somewhat rattled lately. I will tell
you what happened a few days ago which really*

never did sink in to me. A guy took 2 rifles, shot his "mistress," his 14 month old baby, the mother's brother, then shot himself. Nobody would touch the place and somebody thought of me. So I was asked to clean up the place after the bodys were removed. It took me all day and I got a free combo meal from Hardees. No money, no nothin. I guess I really did it for the baby, a beautiful little blond girl.

The talk of Atl. This year has been all about storms. Lots of em. Kinda makes me laugh every time the newspaper says a construction crew or hunter, or whatever, finds a skeleton or corpse and they can't figure out who it is. Well it's a homeless person, that's who it is. That last tornado picked up houses, so whats a little 200 lbs homeless, swhoosh him up and he's a goner.

Thank you for goin on a vacation. You deserved it. I didn't know the U.S. had volcano's. I thout they were in China or Japan.

Butchy

Joye's Notes:

For me, the story of the baby was the most poignant one of the many touching stories Butch told. It is one of those tales that begins sad and just does not let up. While my realities might be dealing with the kid's homework or my problems at work, Butch was right there with murder and death. He spent hours cleaning up a tragedy no one wanted to touch, and they gave him a meal from a fast food place! Who does that? He ought to get a medal. He certainly deserved a decent compensation. I like Hardees, but a combo meal as payment for that job is disgusting. Butch spoke at other times about people asking for his help and repaying him with only a "God Bless You." The Bible warns us about telling poor people to simply be warmed and filled. Maybe a combo meal is better than that, but barely. What is remarkable is Butch's unselfish attitude: "I did it for the baby!"

Butch's comment on the storm exemplifies how his humor always seemed to be there. Of course, the skeleton is from some poor homeless person or a nobody. Swoosh, and he's a goner!

20 I wonder what a wonderful time they're all having

December 2003

Hi family,

I'm just glad you all are my family. The picture is right where I sleep next to dumpster at the QT. Before I had the car given to me, I use to sleep in the dumpster. I do a lot of praying for the car cause it can go anytime.

The 2 girls I told you about, where I use their address, I see them once a week. They are so nice to me and I actually like them, but I don't understand them to save my life. They are pretty and very educated, thats all I know, except that they are married to each other. They keep a lot of secrets.

*All too often I wonder what people "think of me."
You've never met a person who had such a
complex like I did, ha ha. If somebody looked at
me "wrong," I never went near that person again.
Every once in a while I'll pass a house carrying my
cans over my shoulder and the front door will be
open and I'll catch a small look at the tree and
decorations and I wonder what a wonderful time
they're all having. You say a prayer of me.*

*My heart was leapin even before I got your
package, the most beautiful box and gift I ever
received. That vest made me purr like a cat.
Everybody in the Ghetto will be jealous. Love
lifted me,*

2 steppin to Texas,

Butchy

Joye's Notes:

I think I worried most about the cold and am glad
Butch liked the puffer vest. It is too bad everything was lost
each time a vehicle was stolen.

A worker at the QT gas station had a couple of
pictures left on the film roll, so captured Butch's combo
vehicle/house. Butch said he used to sleep in a dumpster, so
a station wagon must have been a step up.

Figure 3 Butch with Cans

    As you can tell, there were many incidences in Butch's life that break my heart. I felt for Butch's lack of family and, in a very small way, tried to give him some connection to ours There were limits, though. It is the holiday seasons that illustrate most the disparities between us. During Christmas, it is not uncommon for 30 family members to crowd into my home to gossip, laugh, and share Italian Cream Cake. I can't help but see Butch pausing in front of an open door, peering in at the presents and tree of a stranger's house, and then walking back to a cold, dark car. How do we draw our circle wider to include the disenfranchised? Is a cup of cold water enough? Are a few letters and an occasional pair of warm gloves sufficient?

21 Something wrong with this world

June 2004

Hi precious,

Your letter hit the spot. You are right to be concerned about Gary's mom. Once they start to get "senile," if you forgive me, it is only a matter of time. 1st thing you know, they will be getting Gary for parental abuse. They would in GA.

You talk about your birds and those pesky squirrels, one day I came back to my truck, it was very cold, and I couldn't get in because a bird got in my truck and I didn't want to frighten it, so I waited till it flew out. At least it wasn't a skunk.

I once told you about the pretty retarded girl I saw and see all the time. For the life of me, I don't know where she lives, or begins her daily wanderings. She will walk past the can recycle place, cross 4 lane hyways. I have saved her more *than once, and yet I know nothing about her! But it has always hurt me inside to see her by herself and seemingly nobody giving a lick! Well last week I was dumpin what cans I collected, I happened to look and she was walking by, with a big bump in front, pregnant! I almost fainted. No man, no ring, no nuthin. Somebody took advantage and will never be seen again. There's something wrong with this world.*

I've had a hard life but I don't cry so much since I met you. I don't understand these con artists who stand at every exit and hold a lying sign begging for money, the same people every day! I'm the only homeless person in Metro Atl who collects cans and never help out my hand one time in my life. All I ever wanted was to be loved and God put you in my life.

Give my love to Gary, Jenna and Wade. I've got her band picture, his baseball picture holdin a bat. I keep them in my Bible. Look at them all the time.

I'm gone,

Butch

Joye's Notes:

Butch's compassion for animals can be seen clearly when he waits patiently in freezing cold for the bird to leave the truck. It is equally on display for humans in his anger at the discovery of the pregnant girl. Butch was generally very sympathetic with fellow street people, although he criticized any able-bodied person who chose to only beg for money. This story and others confirm there is plenty of mental illness in the homeless community, likely worsened by drugs and alcohol. That can and does lead to people being taken advantage of and abused. We can deal easier sometimes with the physical conditions than we can with the mental ones.

Butch and I did share an interest in wildlife and birds. I had told him about a squirrel who kept cleaning out our bird feeder, raking out sunflowers at will. We had built devices to discourage squirrels, but all attempts just seemed to embolden them. Since Gary had a pet squirrel for seven years when he was young, we did not try too hard in our efforts. After all, they are God's creatures also and they loved the free seeds as much as birds do.

We all want to be loved. That is the core of family and friendship. If nothing else, I wanted to show our love for Butch and to encourage him to be optimistic. In return, I got back the same from him.

22 It wasn't much of a life

October 2004

Hi Joye, yippee....it's me Butchy,

I was 14 before I ever saw the inside of a church. Theres a lot of people gone from this life that I will never see again and that was the only life I knew till you helped me find the Lord. And it wasn't much of a life, ha ha. Now I love you and I love Jesus and I am so glad I discover something new. Just 2 days ago I was walkin thru a old property, old apple trees, and on one fence was a big bunch of beautiful red tiny flowers, exactly the shape of stars. I'd never see any before. I was awestruck and I've seen a lot of flowers in my day. Glory to God. I'm probably the only person who saw them.

The ole van I live in is about had it. I've been really blessed with it. I mow for a guy who is a little bit of everything I guess. He has a VW that I can work off so maybe in a couple of months I'll have wheels.

Since I started this letter, I just felt a very heavy burden to check on Miss O'Neal. Every day, 7 days a week without fail, she leaves her cardboard box and pulls her 2 wheel cart to a corner of a parking lot that has a brick made bed for flower plants. She sits there all day in the hot sun, can barely, see, wasted away, maybe 75 lbs. Sweetest person in this sorry city. She was so glad to see me she just hugged and hugged me. She rambled on, of course I never know anything she said, I can't lip read her, no teeth, no distinction between her lips and her face, very aged and neglected. She was wearin a big rain-coat in case it ever rains. I love her and she knows it. I left knowing that someday I will pass that corner and she won't be there.

From the Ghetto,

Love, Butchy

Joye's Notes:

Butch always seemed to get such joy in small things such as star-shaped flowers, perhaps seen by nobody in this world but him.

This Eleanor Rigby-like moment with the frail old lady is a great reminder that the homeless world is populated with all kinds of people in many different situations. Miss O'Neal seems like a poster child for our typical preconceptions. Is she neglected? Or just "is?" "Neglect" implies responsibility. Is she simply no one's responsibility? If so, then whose? Mine? Yours? Government? Church? Someday the world will pass by the corner and she will be....gone.

I do not believe he ever got that Volkswagen.

23 Didn't suffer no more

March 2005

Joye,

I really need to chat with you. It was a rough winter. I was very sick for almost 2 weeks. I wasn't completely well when one of the street folks came to me and told me Mattie died while collectin cans. I mustered enuf strength to go see her at the funeral home. It was the 1st time in my life that I was glad deep inside, that she didn't suffer no more. Of course, I cryed.

I pray you all have a wonderful Easter. I am sorry that I don't know when it is, but I see sales papers and so forth and know its near. It has been on my b'day before. I'm writing with my left hand. Maybe my right hand will stop hurtin in a while. All 4 of my limbs are not what they used to be. But I'm sorry about Gary's fallin ill. Life doesn't seem fair to me.

I usually have something to eat in my van so when I come upon homeless people at the stop lites I'll hand out my food. Those Otis Spunklers Muffins go good. I like to find them. The homeless are woefully rejected here, I ought to know. You would be surprised how many cars kept right on goin past that homeless man I handed food to today right near a mall!

So glad to hear of Wade and Wendi. What a wonderful couple. She could use a few cheeze-burgers but otherwise that smile is so uplifting. And I see Jenna has a beau. What's the deal on that? Has he got $? Otherwise, drop em! That Gary must be 7' tall. Say hello to the cardinals, hummingbirds, squirrels, you name it. I love animals. A big hug for you.

I was at the Motel 6 dumpster 2 days ago where I found your purse. I am glad I was there then. It was pitch dark and another hour and the truck would have come. I would love to place in your hands a beautiful bloomage of wheat sheaves and various plumes made of pure gold symbolizing the scars you healed when I was so destitute.

Please don't pass me by,

Butch

Joye's Notes:

One thing I found that Butch and I have in common is our belief God does work in ways we do not always recognize. I first knew him as just a label, a made-up composite of a poor homeless man. Over time, I learned he was more. He was a human being with a name and emotions just like everyone else. Then, before I realized it, I knew him as a friend who shared with me and taught me about life and faith. What is amazing is that this experience was, in his words, just an hour away from not happening at all. This had to be the hand of God.

Butch always seemed to keep a sense of humor, although I did not pass that cheeseburger comment on to my beautiful future daughter-in-law. Wendi and Wade had just announced their engagement.

It impresses me, that Butch would be collecting and distributing food for the homeless. We commend and appreciate a rich person helping the destitute. Seeing a poor person do the same seems to carry a little more weight and instill a little more guilt in us. This image of Butch illustrates well the story of Jesus and the needy widow. Like Butch, she gave not out of her wealth but did what she could.

24 Never been the same

September 2005

Joye,

I pray this finds you in no way overwhelmed. I know fully well you're taxing yourself more than anybody else. You must be Catholic, ha ha. Poor joke. It is my understanding that most throngs of people from the Gulf Coast relocated to Texas. I did see one sight that will remain with me for a long time. I was traveling toward Atl. and along side em was a big old car loaded with people, the windows were down and we traveled side by side a couple miles. They were like ghosts, lookin straight ahead, no one spoke a word. I could tell they had cryed the whole way from New Orleans. It was like they had came from a funeral. I know the feelin. I wanted to cry but couldn't. There are so many people at the end of their rope today.

I've always been afraid to be normal cause I've known since I was a little boy, how far down *people can fall, and not get back up. That's not for me. As for never been loved or married, that no big deal either. I had a girl friend in 2nd grade named Linda Edsall and then one day, she never came back. 15 years later I'm told that Linda died of polio and nobody wanted to upset me. I've never been the same. But now I realize she is in a better place.*

So, I'm sleeping more now as always when it gets cold. Don't have to go far to the bathroom, just open the van door, amen. I'll be looking for your next letter.

Butchy

Joye's Notes:

The Katrina hurricane of August 2005 had effects over a wide range of states. It speaks to Butch's empathy again when we see him driving down the street and noticing the struggles of others. That ability to pick people out of a situation and feel their pain has been a great lesson for me.

Butch said he never kissed a woman and expressed regret that he would never be married. It was something he could not understand when he saw attractive women with, in his words, the "ugliest" men. What was wrong with him? Was it because he was deaf? His lone encounter with love came from a 2nd-grade crush that ended in tragedy! It is so frustrating to have friends or family who cannot find the life companion they look for. You want to help but understand the often-unfair realities of life.

I know he appreciated our family, but it may have been easy for Butch to wonder why that cannot be him. When we think of homelessness, we tend to think of terms of people without houses. It is also about people without families. "Famililessness," if you please. It is tragic to see people displaced from houses and living in trucks, tents, or in the open. It is equally tragic to realize those same people are displaced from any family and any similar friendship group. Such was the case with Butch. Friends were people he occasionally happened on and then vanished. Any family relationships seemed primarily confined to letters every few weeks from a lady 800 miles away.

25 I walked away with my head down

March 2006

Hi Joye,

Same oh same oh with me. I would go to Fla. in at least Feb. in the winters but I don't know how they treat homeless people. It took me all these years to get "the ropes" down pat so I stay in the good grace of the law and the general public. There is so much cops, paranoid people, sort of living on eggshells in this state. It was just yesterday that I was at a QT and a nice lookin pick-up truck pulls by where I am parked. The "dude," a white guy motions me over, and opens a container and asks me if I want to buy some "Speed." It took him a couple of sec. to realize I was deaf. Then he used his hands "too good" to acknowledge that he sensed I was deaf. But I knew he was a "under-cover." Street people are not that smart.

On another note, even sadder, I told you I collect cans in one trailer park. I am "face" familiar with some of the people. This one old guy has a very precious German Shepherd "Jake" who is now 13 yrs old. I've never met a smarter dog. Unfortunately Jake has arthritis, not much goin for him. But he loves to see me. The guy conveyed to me on my "Eraser Board" that he was having Jake put to sleep. I walked away with my head down.

Write when your frantic pace slows down.

Butchy

Joye's Notes:

Even his friendships with animals, whether with pets owned by other people or with stray cats he fed, were temporary. In one sense, all relationships here on earth do not last, but for the homeless they seem shorter. In Butch's case, most relationships seemed to rest with the other side and were outside of his control.

He speaks of trying to stay in the good grace of the law and of being approached by an undercover cop looking to entrap him. How many of us live in that environment? Certainly, there are groups of people like the homeless or some minorities who stay in that world, caught between fearing the police and fearing strange people. Fortunately, in this case, the policeman was after different targets and recognized Butch's situation quickly. Although a real problem was averted, it still is very uncomfortable being constantly suspected by outsiders. I can imagine being deaf and I can imagine being homeless, but it is hard to imagine how frightening it is to be both.

As for my frantic pace, Butch was referring to my work in a CPA office during tax season.

26 Stupid

August 2006

Everyone,

No more "Jake." I miss seeing him, but like you said, he isn't suffering no more.

Whoa this has been a scorcher. If the other torching states are in the same boat as GA, I really feel for them. Can u believe, people still stupid enuf to leave a child in a car! I thot people quit doin that. I know how hot it is sleeping in my van with the windows down and no back window.

Just 2 weeks ago, and it was "HOT," I agreed to clear out (trash everything) the compiling of 10 yrs worth of filth and neglect in a old hermits trailer who died. The dump wouldn't even take the trailer. I knew he was, well, not actually retarded, but things obviously happened in his life, and he went off the radar, holed up in that trailer with ? cats, and never took the trash out or "lived" all the space. I bagged bags full of cobwebs. All that work for $15. But I said to myself, "That's where I came from, this could have been me." I've been in that situation so many times, now when I see a truck backed up to a house, I run. All people do is use me. I even get asked at dumpsters to carry a mattress or whatever, "please, to my apartment," "God bless you." Whatever.

Now how bout Bro. Gary? Is there anything they can do for his ulcers? I don't know why I'm still alive, ha ha. I used to go thru this eviction junk on curbs so forth, and I would always see bottles of herbs, all kinds of "natural" junk and I would take pills and not even know what they were for. Stupid. I stopped doin that long time ago. I thot I was drinkin from da fountain of youth. Most of the stuff was woefull.

Where your road leads, I will follow.

Butchy

Joye's Notes:

Oh, Butch loved that dog, Jake. He still mentions him, years later. At times like this when he experiences a lonely loss, I wish I could give Butch a hug. Letters can express some feelings but are poor substitutes for personal interaction.

Butch had different vehicles. He usually owned junkers someone had given him. Those various cars or trucks were all likely on their last legs or last wheels. He would drive them until they would not go anymore. Sometimes they were stolen before their final demise. A van or station wagon had some advantages over a truck for living space. Remember, a truck cab is a relatively small living space. An occupant cannot stand or even stretch out to sleep. We had some friends who sold their house and moved into a tiny house. Listening to them talk about life in a 400-foot house was fascinating to me. How many square feet of floor space is there in a pickup cab? Combine that with no heat, no electricity, no appliances, no washer, no stove, no TV, and no computer No, thanks.

When Butch did complain, it was mostly about the cold. Similarly, the heat in Atlanta must at times be stifling. And no, Butch, there seems to be no expiration date for stupidity. Texas must lead the nation in kids left in hot cars.

27 Do they make a sound?

August 2006

Hi Pal,

I'm still "truckin" and holdin up quite well. You know since I quit coffee a few years ago, I don't feel the heat so much. I used to practically heave under the heat. I've cut back on the cappacunni too, and I love that stuff. But I find lots of Gatorade, energy drinks, pour in a clean bottle and really peps me up.

I told you about that "dump" trailer park that I go in, collect cans, check on a coon dog that loves me, mow for a few that are unable to, for a couple bucks. I went to the door and the lady partly opened it, handed me a couple dollars, and I walked away thinking, "Gee, she didn't look too good." In 2 hours, she is dead! Heatstroke. I felt bad but I never "impose." If she had handed me a note and said "I need help," I would have jumped on it right there!

It's gonna cool off soon. There's already been a lot of wildlife on the move like deer. I've seen fox, bobcat, Canadian geese, coons, all kinda stuff. I found a big ole air conditioner (junk) and I thot I'll tear it apart and try to get a couple dollars at the recycle. I turned it over and out came a great big rat, thru my legs, and disappeared not realizing that I was the one scared to death.

Hows all your friends around the yard doin, the birds, turtles, rabbits, etc. I saw a wild turkey the other morning on the way to recycle. I tried to scare it back into the woods so no idiot get any ideas. I shot a blue jay when I was a young boy and I have never forgiven myself. I was so excited last week, I got real close to a hummingbird. I was so thrilled even tho I couldn't hear it. Do they make a sound?

Happy Anniversary.

Butchy

Joye's Notes:

I empathize with Butch's regret at shooting the blue jay. I do not condemn hunters nor am I a vegan, but I do not personally grasp killing animals for the fun of it. I would not even consider putting a worm on a hook just so I can snag a fish with the same hook. I just feel too sorry for the worm!

It breaks my heart to hear Butch ask if hummingbirds make a sound. There is so much we can take for granted. Butch was not always deaf, but likely he did not remember hummingbirds from his youth. He has related to me about not hearing the gospel singing on TV, the rain at night, bees before they sting him, sermons at church, and, of course, every other person he meets. Writing letters must give Butch a great outlet for communication with another person he seldom enjoys otherwise.

He was sweet to remember our anniversary.

28 *I was nobodys favorite*

December 2007

Dearest Joye,

I like to read old books. Do you realize, and I'm not pulling your leg, somewhere in my lineage was a great aunt or, I don't honestly know how she got in the Russell family. But her name was Aunt Mildred Lincoln-Todd, and she was a descendant of President Lincoln. I did know my cousin Johnny Todd, he was killed in Viet-Nam. I really loved that boy. So I keep up with the past more than the present. I remember my grandmother who lived in a old trailer in a field, and I would take her a apple or see her up close lots of times, and I never ever saw her lips move!

Its not an easy life, but in my case, its basically the only life I've ever known. You know all that. I tell you truthfully, with no bad feelings toward anyone, I was nobodys favorite. More than one coach and teacher hit me. All long forgotten But it makes me feel good I know someone like you.

I'd like to have a chain and a cross for Christmas to wear around my neck. I always wanted one.

This is a more "Christmasy" season than it was last year. Lots of people are decorating their yards, trees up, on and on. People are realizing the "time" they have on this earth is more precious, than they thought it was. Fate is carooming all over this country. Not even safe in a church. I want you to assure me that Jenna and Wendi are packin some kind of heat. You know how depressed I once was and just couldn't snap out of "offences" done to me. So you prayed that I would be "happy" and I am, and I always want you to be proud of me.

Butchy

Joye's Notes:

I doubt Jenna and Wendi ever "packed heat" at church or anywhere else, but I can appreciate the concern for their safety. There are real dangers out there, even in houses of worship Not that long ago, several people were killed at a nearby church building, one Gary had visited before.

Butch asked for so little and was always appreciative of any small Christmas gift. It was difficult for me to think of something that might be appropriate for his situation. A few weeks earlier, I had asked Butch what he might like, and he only mentioned the cross and chain. I guess there is something poetic about a person only wanting the Cross. I am glad he liked it.

29 I never hear the words "I love you"

January 2009

Dear Precious Joye,

How are you? What a way to start a letter to you with! It's usually you asking me. But you know I love writing to you, although I have to wear powerful glasses and I don't use my thumb to write.

Your so right. That little "Jesse" is adorable. This baby has taken my spirit to a whole new level and Jenna is gonna be a wonderful mother. You will have myriad of ways to fill your days. Lots of picture albums comin' up, memories that will just spontaneously unfold, humming with the birds, rocking the baby.

The past couple months they have been payin pretty good at recycle. I get excited every time I find anything at the dumpsters. The more weight the better. I go to the recycle twice a wk, bout 50 a load. So $100 a wk ain't bad. It takes a lot of dumpsters, complexes, hour after hour, day to nite, to fill a load up, and I hardly ever have a full load. I get very choked up sometimes.

It's going to take a few days of "'sunshine" for me to snap out of all this head-aches, all kinds of blahs, cold, almost miserable. It has rained for days, non-stop. And a week ago, I was snowed in at the QT. Never moved. Hardest snow I ever seen in GA. So I'm prayin hard for some sunshine. Probably heard about the guy that jumped off Niagara Falls and "survived," and tried to stop people from rescuing him, he wanted to die. I've been there, done that.

To this day, I have yet to see another person in a dumpster, or arrive to a dumpster and see a bag torn or any showing that anybody was there. Just me in all of Atl. and I hit dumpsters every day, hour after hour! Cans are only 25 cents a pound. But I'm happy. You don't see me at a traffic stop begging. I never hear the words "I love you" but you always tell that by your letters.

I still think about those 3 sisters on a church program like your church, sang with no music.

They glowed; I was so glad that I saw them. Those 3 precious sisters were only interested in being a blessing. They never mentioned money. If this country was reduced to soup lines and 2 days a wk electricity, those men and women preachers on T.V. would still beg people for their last dime.

I've had a long day. I'm gonna lay across the seat and plan tomorrow, what dumpsters to hit.

Love,

Butch

Joye's Notes:

Butch did not discuss politics too much, but it was clear there were many elected officials he cared little about. The same could be said of televangelists.

From his photo, I knew he sometimes wore glasses. Once, he even said he was going to get some free glasses. However, I did not know how bad his eyes were until this letter. One more problem!

I try to send him photos of our family each Christmas. Here is one of our family Christmas photographs including Gary, Joye, Jenna, Wendi, and Wade. Of course, the first grandson Jesse was our pride and joy. We now have five precious grandsons.

Figure 4 Joye with Family

I was glad that Butch could feel like he was a part of our family, even though the connection was only through the mail. In our life, we have so many different relationships. What I share with Butch is unusual in some ways. At times, I wondered if there should be more, such as a face-to-face meeting. We have never met Butch nor invited him into our house. Part of that could just be chalked up to "life happens" as it always seemed we were busy. Part of the problem is simple logistics. For example, would we drive to Atlanta and eat lunch in his pickup cab? Another part is the realization that we can try to reach across the divides and relate to other people, but there are limitations also. Trying to pull someone out of their context and make them into your image is not always best for either party. I felt that we have a unique friendship that started with a chance letter sent by Butch. We could share, we could encourage, we could reach out in love as one child of God to another. Would another step beyond that be beneficial? Even possible? Anyone, whether that be a social worker or a missionary, struggles with how to help the disadvantaged. Sometimes the best help is not to radically change a person's culture to ours but to be there for them in theirs. For me, Butch was not a charity case. He was simply a friend who happened to live in another culture.

30 Lord, I'm comin' home

April 2010

Hi Joye, Jesse, Jenna,

I sometimes wonder what I'm missing in seeing people on cell phones all the time, lap tops, all kinds of technology. You've been so kind to write to me. The part about pickin cotton was enlightening. It was probably when I was in my late 20's when I begin to realize there was a Texas. I guess that may be a little difficult for you to understand.

God has been a real protector, like you said. For me, many times. I have never forgotten the 2 times I've been hit by cars crossing a street and never saw them coming. I'm amazed I've lived all these years. Those were "little" potatoes compared to other close calls.

It was a rough winter for me but nothing compared to my coon dog dying just before my birthday. Nobody ever loved me like that dog. It will be a long time if ever I get over her. I could get into a good argument with JOB if I could talk, and to think God gave him back. I dug a grave out in the woods and I wanted to die right there. I opened your card and the pictures of the dog lifted my spirit.

I was surprised to see a man at a red light begging, like they do in lot of places. He was pulling along a big air tank, oxygen so he could breathe. Wow. I've seen everything day after day. I save all the can food I find and take it to a homeless shelter. I've took 2 big boxes in one week. I remember Gov. Jimmy Davis, he sang a song, "Someone, somewhere, may knock on your door, someone who needs a loving hand; someone you've never met before; someone who will always be your friend."

Not too many people get along now days. Deep down in my heart I care about other people. I don't even need money to live. That's why I kinda scratched my head when you said this is the richest country. I don't know anything about "rich" and I certainly don't envy whoever? One time years ago, it was a dark night, I was going on *a back country road. I was passin a black church that had a cemetery behind it. I saw 4 guys carrying a body bag with a body inside, and they buried the guy without a casket. I'm sure it was all legal, it was a funeral home. But apparently, no money for anything else. I probably won't even make it that far, just lay down somewhere where I will never be found, and "Lord, I'm comin home."*

From the ghetto,

Butchy

Joye's Notes:

When we are going through hardships, one of the added anxieties often relates to how long the suffering will last. We might bravely tell ourselves we can endure anything if we know there is an end. Many of us are particularly hopeful that all difficulties will result in a fair outcome. Butch is right. While the story of Job encourages us during periods of trial, it must be admitted Job ultimately experienced some type of compensatory restitution. We do not always obtain a similar satisfaction. What is it like when we can see no hope or feel we cannot dream of any just resolution? What if we saw our destination as simply lying down without ever being found?

Butch noted he never heard of Texas until he was in his late 20s. That is hard for me to picture. Still, it is always insightful to see how much Butch could be off the grid concerning things that seem so common to me.

What would we do without cell phones or Facebook? I am not sure what Butch has missed in the tech department, but we might all remember how our life shuts down when the electricity goes down for a few hours.

31 I bleed French Vanilla

March 2012

My Joye,

1st your hand, now your ankle. You are certainly
not alone there in your w. chair. You have no idea
the close calls I've had that could have left me
paralyzed. Maybe a yr. or so before I "met" you, I
suffered a terrible "deep gash" on my left foot,
about 3" up in the back from the flat sole. It was
a stupid thing I did inside a dumpster. I managed
to climb out, and I knew my best bet was to get to
the "Elizabeth Inn," a homeless ministry one exit
away. I was bleeding bad. As soon as I got there,
they rushed me to the hospital. I had 2 or 3 straph
infections. That whole debacle lasted a long time,
all because I stomped on a big thick glass to get a
aluminum can!

Now it can't get hot enuf for me. I've even
noticed my feet have no tingling. Might be
because I quit drinking those energy drinks from

QT fountain. Wow, they must be loaded with sugar. I'm a slow learner but God finally got thru my head. But I could never give up my cappacunie (can't spell it). I have a 52 oz. mug, ha ha! If I cut my finger, I bleed French Vanilla.

Wow, the Rangers are loaded. Because of you, I've grown to be excited about them. I'm sick of the Yankees anyways!

The sweater is more than I deserved. You will not believe how many coats I've seen in dumpsters every year, but rarely a sweater.

Hope you had a Happy Valentines,

Butchy

Joye's Notes:

I had broken my hand and then my foot, three months apart. The latter surgery left me in a wheelchair for a while. Butch's story illustrates that homeless ministries do provide many needed services, although everyone realizes how basic those provisions are.

Most of the letters I wrote to Butch seemed boring to me. It was impossible to come up with something profound to say every time. Usually with people in our lives we simply want to talk about the weather or what happened yesterday. Here is a typical letter from me to Butch:

March 7, 2012

Dear Butch,

I hope this letter finds you doing well. That was quite a story you told me in your last letter when you cut your foot so badly. God was really looking out for you on that one. I do hope you are more careful now....right?

We continue to have spring weather. Gary mowed this week for the first time since last fall.

You talked about having relatives that you don't even know. That is true for me also. My mother had six brothers and sisters and most of them had a lot of kids...one had twelve kids. Since I am the youngest of seven kids for my mother that makes me a lot younger than MANY of my first cousins. I think I told you that my mother's grandmother was full blood Chickasaw Indian. She came from Mississippi on the Trail of Tears. A lot of my cousins look very Indian with black hair and very dark eyes.

I think that your being able to read lips is a very interesting thing. I am so thankful that you can since most people can't sign with you. You can understand TV that way, too.

Yes, our Rangers are loaded up! They are really trying to get back to the World Series again. Maybe it is in the cards one more time.

Well, that is about all I know.

Love,

Joye

32 My people died long ago

July 2012

Dearest Joye,

Please forgive me taking so long to write. Better if you do not worry about me. I will never tell you what I've been through. I didn't even tell you everything about that big gash. Oh my!

I'm goin to be honest with you; I didn't know any better. I had a hard time startin out homeless. My people died long ago. I still feel bad that my mother died in a institution, and they notified me a year later. I certainly never got over my baby sister when she died in her sleep takin a nap, crib death. I left N.Y. when about 23 but I sure was scared. There was nothin for me to live there. It was a living hell. I came to GA., fell in love with the sunshine. I was shocked when you 1st wrote me.

Well I pace myself with the heat. I find bottles of water in QT dumpsters, add ice, feels good. Never had a problem up until a week ago. I dumped the water in the ice, took a big gulp, and it was vodka or something else. I am more careful now. In the Civil War they called it the "Joy Drink." You are my Joy.

Until next time,

Butch

Joye's Notes:

I received a letter in April 2012 but then went several months without hearing from Butch. That was unusual and more worrisome as the days passed with no word. He had no phone and I had little contact information. I was always concerned that something would happen to Butch and he would simply disappear. He had said one of the times he was hit by a car he had been thrown over the hood and was taken to a hospital. And earlier in this year, he described a severe foot injury he once had. I was starting to think of how I might have to try to find him when this letter arrived in July. Of course, I was happy he was still alive. However, it gave me no comfort when he declined to divulge the mysterious event in his life. I never found out what that might have been.

33 A good pair of sunglasses

November 2012

Momma Joye,

I been meaning to write. A chance came up to come to Fla. This will be the biggest challenge of my life. I told you once that my sister had done a lot of traveling and she had these friends. They have been very nice to me and I'm using their address. I got tired of Atl. I'll try to get started recycling, maybe even "collect trash" for people, mow lawns, and try to capture some alligators.

I'm learning this area slowly. I've hit a few dumpsters. Just like ole times. I could win the lottery and I'd still jump in dumpsters. And this is great to sleep outside. Even better than GA. it took me up to now to realize I couldn't keep driving such long distances every day in GA like I did yr. in, yr. out and never made a dime. And the

2 girls at the recycle were always taking 5-10 dollars from me for "tip", every time I went. I didn't have the heart to stop it. Down here I don't even have to drive. Its all civilization, nonstop.

It's a whole new world to me but it is very beautiful. I now get a little social security and food stamps and I don't have to kill myself. I walk up and down the shoreline staring at the boats. I had never seen sand before. Birds walk right up to me. Life is good and yes, I do sleep in my truck. I'll probably be here 5 yrs before I make a friend. Its just so difficult being deaf. I think I can make it here. I just need a good pair of sunglasses and the nerve to wear shorts.

Until next time,

Butch

Joye's Notes:

Butch had mentioned before about the possibility of moving to Florida or some other warm state like Texas. Still, I was surprised to get a letter with Tampa/St. Petersburg as the return address. The details of the relocation were murky, but he took the opportunity when he could. I was glad to see him get out of the Georgia winters and to start a new life. The food stamps and social security would definitely be helpful to him.

Some people might consider this pen-pal relationship between a happily married suburbanite and a homeless single man to be unusual. Even though he called me Momma in this letter, I know Butch might have wished for more at times. After all, he occasionally said we should run away and get married. However, he also said the same about women he saw on T.V. A couple of times he asked if I had a sister! We are friends and there is nothing more than that. But that is saying a lot. Friendships come in many forms. I can honestly say Butch is a closer friend than many of my "hi and how are you?" acquaintances.

34 Amen, brother

December 2015

Thank you, Joye!

That album was amazing. I will cherish that album always and when I die, its goin with me. I'm the only one that's got gray hair! You and Gary still look like kids. Is it the water? I wished you would marry me.

This area fits me nice. Slowly I'm coming out of my life-time shell and I ride my bike a lot. Oh my, this is big time bike riding heaven. I got 2 libraries I can ride my bike to so I enjoy looking. And I love to fish. I go to church, have never heard a sermon, I just like to go. I've got a few lawn customers. Hope I get more. I've been blessed, thank the Lord.

Just got back from the Food Bank. Wow, never seen it that crowded before. My cousin chatted with a young girl who is a 'stripper." You would *think they make good money. Saw a homeless guy with a T-shirt, said "My Family Tree is Full of Nuts." Amen, brother, your alrite! I saw on T. V. where people take pictures of homeless people sleeping, so forth, to "shame" them. What's this country comin to?*

Love always,

Butch

Joye's Notes:

Over the years, I sent Butch several family pictures. For this Christmas, I made a family photo album, with individual pictures of my husband and me, our children, their spouses, and even the grandsons. Everybody included a note to Butch. Just as Butch thought of himself as a part of our family, I wanted our family to have a connection also.

I was happy for him to have some relationship with a church, although that is often difficult for a new deaf person. I hoped and prayed that someone there would reach out to Butch in a personal way. It would be inexcusable if Butch felt ignored. It is so easy in a church for members to spend time only with friends or other people who are like them.

35 Everything I owned

July 2017

Dear Joye,

I don't have any money yet here in Fla. But I'm very happy and I see good things happening in the future. I ride my bike to a church. I wish I could understand but just goin makes me feel good. I lean forward if someone speaks to me, and imagine what their voice sounds like. I am good at it and because I am probably the best lip-reader in America, I try to get as much as I can out of each service. I really love it. They got a nice gathering place to drink coffee and all kinds of brekfast stuff. I'm gonna mow some lawns for them old people. There's only way to go in this beautiful area—up. The more I think about it, I feel its all Gods timing.

The recycle days are over. But actually they were more or less over in GA. I used to collect so many cans I hid bags full everywhere. Thousands and thousands of them. At least I still go behind stores and get food. The church has a homeless ministry. There is a big table where people donate food. If I find real good stuff I take it and leave it on the table but nobody knows. I know they are using it and it makes me feel like I'm a blessing.

Just going a winter without a cold is gold to me. This house here is 30+ years old. I sleep on the floor but that's the way I am. I don't like beds. I never dreamed my life would end up in Fla. so I'm hoping the good Lord has something in store for me around here. My cousin Charlotte here was my aunt Alice and uncle Sherman pride and joy. They must have told her to look after me before they passed. She is a wonderful person but I worry to myself about her health.

I lost so much when my trucks were stolen in Atl. Everything I owned was in those trucks including Tammy Faye Bakkers own personal bible she sent me. Her son was a homeless minister in Atl. I was homeless for many yrs. Still am in a way. So when you sent me that bible, I couldn't think straight. You have been nothing but good to me. Thank *you dear Joye for wishin me a good year. I know I will because I have a wonderful friend like you.*

The fish are callin me. I don't have any bait but people usually give me some by the bridge. The best part is watchin the dolphins play. But them pelicans pester me to death, standin right next to me like I'm Spencer Tracy or sometin. Gimme a break. I just wanna catch come fish to eat.

Have a great week,

Butch

Joye's Notes:

Early on, I sent Butch a Bible before I knew he had any. Later, he said he found Bibles all the time in the trash. I am not sure what that says about us. I was happy to send a few things to ease his life but knowing how much and what could be hard. I knew he liked to read, but he had so little space in a truck cab for anything but himself. The back of the truck was used for cans.

It appeared that life in Florida suited him. I could tell the warmer weather, the access to libraries and fishing, and some connection to church and family gave him more peace. Not having to rely on collecting cans eased his life considerably as it was such a hard job. I am not sure he ever got up the nerve to wear shorts!

36 Praise the Lord

April 2020

My best friend, Joye,

Yea!! You are well. Praise the Lord.

I have no problem "isolating," "distancing"—so on. I stay in my room "garage" hours on end. Don't bother me and I never interact with people anyways. Didn't even do that at church. I couldn't belive (actually I could) that some churches here were still holdin services.

2019 went by fast. I learned a lot of sign language. I will tell you bout the "church" sometime. I'm not "happy" with the "things" I see—people comin and goin. A deaf person will come, they won't stay. It hurts. Every deaf person is different. I get attached to some of them in just one meeting, then poof—they gone. That's all I've ever known all my life.

I just saw a elderly person on a 3 wheel bike—lots of them around, but this one also has a "motor." The only time I drive my cousins car is to run a errand for her. I don't even care to drive. But that 3 wheel "motor" bike has really got me thinking, with a big basket on the back. Yes, I remember that fool driving—not even looking, and hit me. Of course, that was in GA—here I would own his house ha, ha.

I definitely ride my bike so I can observe all my animals. I see lots of big—like hawks—vultures, and my ospreys. And I went fishin a little bit—the water is 100? yards from here. I almost threw my line right on top of a alligator. I oughta write a book, ha, ha—dedicated to you.

I'm still keepin up with baseball. TX sure does love their baseball. I think they will pay you to go to Tampa Bay Rays games.

So glad that all the grandkids are doing fine. They have a wonderful Nana.

Love,

Butch

Joye's Final Notes:

I am happy to hear Butch is surviving this crazy Covid 19 mess. I guess he was isolating already.

The story is not finished, because we are still writing! I think Butch's homeless years are mostly behind him, although he remains homeless in some ways. He has been united with a cousin and has a real roof over his head, despite

continuing to sleep on a garage floor. I am not sure he has ever given up visits to the dumpster for some food. He does fish a lot more, which gives him hot fresh food. This past Christmas I sent him some fishing lures and hooks. Perhaps it was one of them he tossed at the alligator.

Figure 5 Butch in Florida

Yes, Butch could write a book. For many years, I wanted to share his life with others, so they could get to know him as I do. There were always questions about how much to interfere in the life of another person. As it is, most books are never read and slip quickly into obscurity. On the other hand, the subject of a book could become known and exposed to potential risks or intrusions. I wanted Butch's opinion, so I did get his permission. He was thrilled at the prospect of a book. I hope this does one him justice!

In many ways, Butch fits our notions of what it means to be on the streets. In other ways, he is a unique individual and is much more than a "homeless person." He is a very thoughtful and considerate person who has shared with me his highs, his lows, and his sustaining faith. Over the years, Butch addressed me with a litany of colorful names such as Mama, Pal, Friend, Dearest, Darling, or Precious. Maybe my favorite one is still "My best friend Joye."

Acknowledgments

I AM GRATEFUL to all the people who encouraged me in bringing this book to life. I am especially indebted to Cassie Bullock, Pat Ming, Jan Rogers, Marylee Ross, and Janice Wright who took the time to supply invaluable critique and suggestions. Of special note is my husband, Gary. Without his support and help there would have been no book.

About the Author

JOYE HOLMES grew up one of seven children in an Oklahoma farming community. After serving as a missionary in Brazil, she enjoyed a long career as an accountant. Her debut book *Somebody Someday: A Journey of Homelessness, Faith, & Friendship* is a true story that grew out of a twenty-five-year correspondence.

Joye lives in Mansfield, Texas with her husband, Gary, where she spends time enjoying five grandsons, her time at church, needlework, and the Texas Rangers.

Connect with the Author

I hope you enjoyed reading this book and getting to know Butch. You may want to connect with me at joye@firemountainpublishing.com. All your comments and corrections will be taken seriously. I look forward to hearing from you!

Please click five stars on Amazon or, better yet, post an honest review. Reviews can be given on Amazon, www.firemountainpublishing.com, or any other site where you bought this book. I would be very grateful. Your support makes a difference.

Made in the USA
Las Vegas, NV
13 September 2021